TO

_____

FROM

_____

DATE

_____

Shine Bright Every Day: Sparkling Reflections of You
Copyright © 2017 by DaySpring
ISBN: 978-1-68408-114-1

Published by:

P.O. Box 1010
Siloam Springs, AR 72761
dayspring.com

Editorial Director: Erin Helmer
Designer: Jessica Wei
Lettering Artists: Morgan Ankrom, Taylor Bogle, Caylie Foley, Daniel Herron, Emily Hesslen, Alisa Hipp,
    Andrea Howey, Jon Huckeby, Greg Jackson, Maryanne Frawley, Jessica Wei

Shine Bright

EVERY DAY

Sparkling Reflections of You

LIVE TODAY WITH joy

THIS IS THE DAY THAT
THE LORD HAS MADE;
LET US REJOICE
AND BE GLAD IN IT.

PSALM 118:24 ESV

The LORD will fulfill
his purpose for me;

your

steadfast

love

O LORD, endures forever.

PSALM 138:8 ESV

Always remember, your life has a purpose that God will fulfill.

Vulnerability isn't weakness;

it's strength.

That's why I take pleasure
in my weaknesses, and
in the insults, hardships,
persecutions, and troubles
that I suffer for Christ.
For when I am weak,
then I am strong.

II CORINTHIANS 12:10 NLT

My cup

overflows.

PSALM 23:5 NLT

I have loved you
with an everlasting love;
Therefore, I have drawn you
with loving-kindness.

JEREMIAH 31:3 NASB

Perfectly imperfect... and completely loved.

YOU WILL FILL ME WITH

joy

IN YOUR PRESENCE.

PSALM 16:11 NIV

BE BEAUTIFUL INSIDE, IN YOUR HEARTS.

I PETER 3:4 TLB

TRUE BEAUTY IS ON THE INSIDE.

Be the
real deal.

Clothe yourselves with *compassion, kindness, humility, gentleness* and *patience.*

COLOSSIANS 3:12 NIV

BROKEN BUT *beautiful.*

My grace is sufficient for you, for my POWER is made perfect in weakness.

2 CORINTHIANS 12:9 NIV

Love
well

Pursue Love.

1 Corinthians 14:1 NASB

EXPRESS YOUR FAITH

THROUGH LOVE.

WHAT IS IMPORTANT IS

faith

EXPRESSING ITSELF IN

love.

GALATIANS 5:6 NLT

God's love
has been poured out
into our hearts.

ROMANS 5:5 NIV

She was

brave

on the inside,

where God does

beautiful

things.

You desire
truth
in the
inner parts.

PSALM 51:6 NASB

God takes
ordinary
and makes it
extraordinary.

Now to Him
who is able to do
far more abundantly
beyond all that
we ask or think,
according to the power
that works within us,
to Him be the glory.

EPHESIANS 3:20–21 NASB

His divine power

has given us everything we need

for a godly life.

II PETER 1:3 NIV

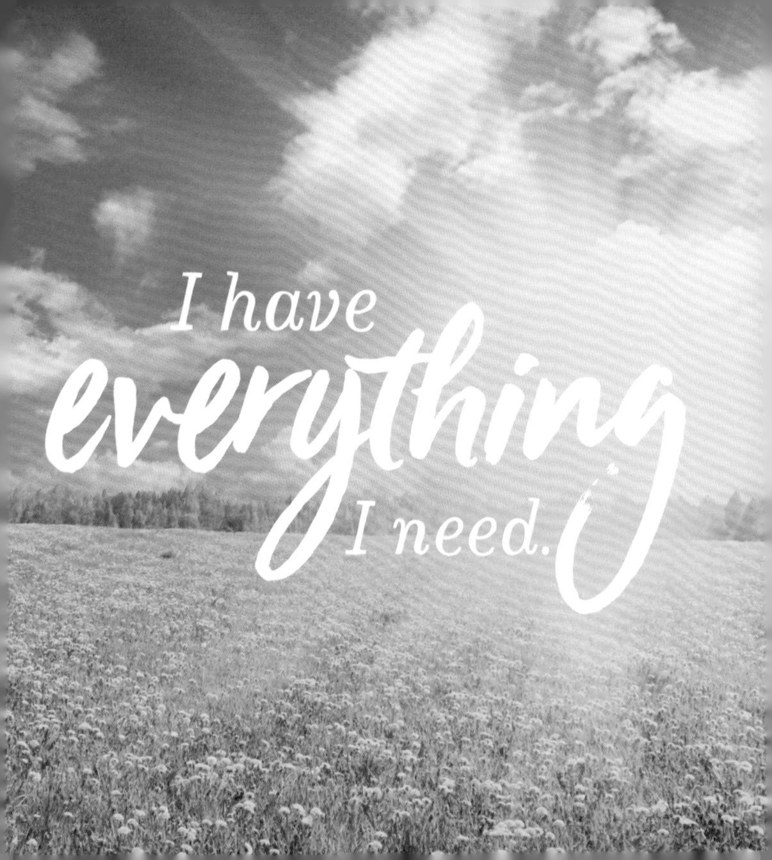
I have
everything
I need.

THE ONLY
THING THAT
TRULY
SATISFIES
IS THE
Love
OF CHRIST.

Satisfy us each morning

with your unfailing love,

so we may sing for joy

to the end of our lives.

PSALM 90:14 NLT

Authentic love finds its source in God.

GOD IS
Love
I JOHN
4:16

Then you will know
the truth,
and the truth will set
you free.

JOHN 8:32 NIV

God knew you first,

knows you best,

and loves you most.

O Lord,
You have searched
me and known
me.

PSALM 139:1 NASB

The Lord...makes us

more and more like Him

as we are changed into

His glorious image.

II CORINTHIANS 3:18 NLT

Called

Gifted

Loved

Even before
He made the world,
God loved us
and chose us.

EPHESIANS 1:4 NLT

Surely I am with you always

MATTHEW 28:20
NIV

God is
always
with me.

Wholly loved

with

holy love.

Let the beloved
of the Lord
rest secure
in Him.

DEUTERONOMY 33:12 NIV

THE ONLY *wealth* THAT MATTERS IS BEING RICH *in Christ.*

True humility and
fear of the LORD lead
to riches, honor,
and long life.

PROVERBS 22:4 NLT

You are fearfully
and wonderfully made—
don't ever forget it!

I praise You because I am fearfully and wonderfully made.

PSALM 139:14 NIV

Everything beautiful

BEGINS WITH GOD.

He has made
everything beautiful
in its time.

ECCLESIASTES 3:11 NIV

YOU BRING GOD'S BEAUTIFUL

LIGHT TO THE WORLD—

Let it shine!

LET YOUR LIGHT SHINE.

MATTHEW 5:16 NIV

LIVING BY FAITH IS LIFE'S GREATEST ADVENTURE.

The LORD says,
"I will guide you along
the best pathway
for your life…"

PSALM 32:8 NLT

You have the power of

God's love

within you and all
of heaven ahead of you.

For God has not given us a spirit of fear, but of power and of love and of a sound mind.

II TIMOTHY 1:7 NKJV

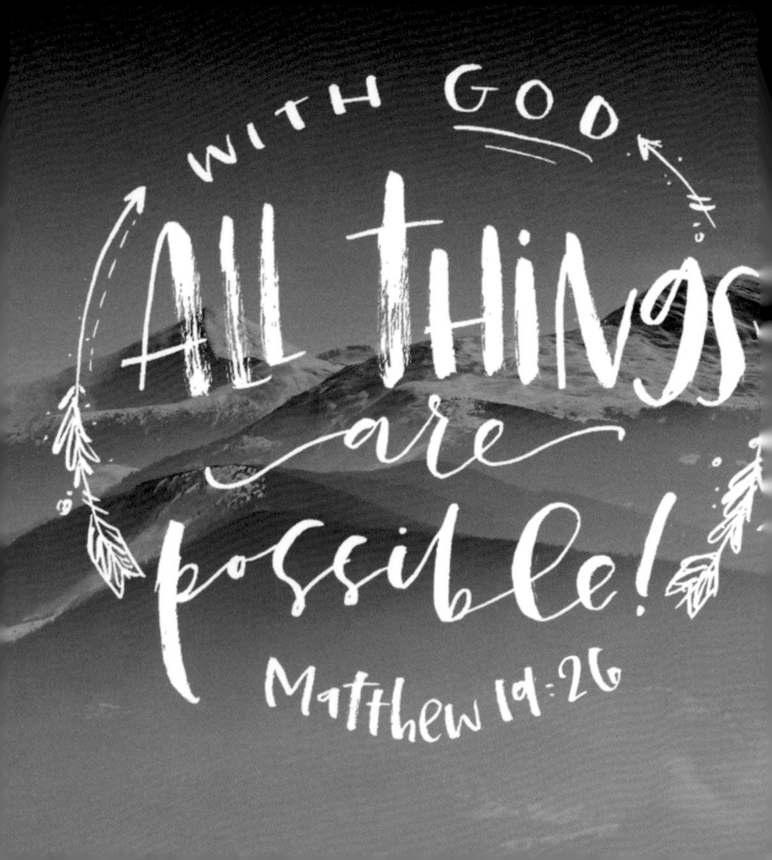
With God
All things
are
possible!
Matthew 19:26

There are

NO LIMITS

to what

YOU AND GOD

can do

TOGETHER!

The God of love and peace will be with you.

II CORINTHIANS 13:11 NIV

TODAY YOU ARE
SURROUNDED BY
God's love
& BLESSED BY
HIS PEACE.

The LORD will work out
His plans for my life—
for Your faithful love,
O LORD, endures forever.

PSALM 138:8 NLT

Explore

the width, length,

height, and depth of

God's great love

for you.

May you have the power

to understand...

how wide, how long,

how high, and how deep

His love is.

EPHESIANS 3:18 NLT

You are

valued

& loved

just because you're you!

You are *precious* to Me.

You are *honored,*

and I *love you.*

ISAIAH 43:4 NLT

*Every
good thing
is a gift
from God.*

Every good and
perfect gift is
from above,
coming down from
the Father.

JAMES 1:17 NIV

LOVE WILL NEVER END
BECAUSE OF GOD'S
never-ending love.

The steadfast love
of the Lord is from
EVERLASTING TO EVERLASTING.

PSALM 103:17 NRSV

If God
says it,
you can
TRUST it.

Yes, I will trust
the promises of God.

PSALM 56:3 TLB

Celebrate

*every great thing
the Lord is doing
in and through
your life.*

The Lord has done
great things for us, and we are
filled with joy.

PSALM 126:3 NIV

You
are precious to Me.

You are honored,

and I love you.

ISAIAH 43:4 NLT

TODAY HAS

God loves you

WRITTEN ALL OVER IT!

Let your day
rest in God's hands
& enjoy where
He takes you.

You alone are my God;

my times are in Your hands.

PSALM 31:14 TLB

*The blessing of the L*ORD

makes a person rich.

PROVERBS 10:22 NLT

Experience god's best in everything!

I have loved you...
with an everlasting love.

JEREMIAH 31:3 NLT

GOD LOVES YOU
LIKE CRAZY...
AND THAT WILL
NEVER CHANGE.

Everywhere you go,

the love and presence

of God go with you.

THE FAITHFUL LOVE OF THE

Lord

NEVER ENDS!

LAMENTATIONS 3:22 NLT

ENJOY YOUR DAY

TO THE FULLEST
and find
GOD'S GOODNESS
IN EVERY PART OF IT.

Surely Your goodness

and unfailing love

will pursue me

all the days of my life.

PSALM 23:6 NLT

SEE HOW VERY MUCH
OUR FATHER
— LOVES US, —
FOR HE CALLS US
His children.

I JOHN 3:1 NLT

— YOU ARE —

completely loved

— BY THE —

Creator

— OF THE UNIVERSE. —

BELIEVE IN THE *power* OF *prayer*, AND THE *faithfulness* OF OUR AMAZING, ALL-POWERFUL GOD.

HEAR MY PRAYER,
O LORD...
ANSWER ME BECAUSE
YOU ARE FAITHFUL.

PSALM 143:1 NLT

The best dreams
are the ones
God has in His heart
for you.

No mind has imagined what God has prepared for those who love Him.

I CORINTHIANS 2:9 NLT

Because Your love
is better than life,
my lips will glorify You.

PSALM 63:3 NIV

All the days ordained for me were written in Your book before one of them came to be.

PSALM 139:16 NIV

God fills YOUR EVERY CHAPTER *with the plans* HE HAS WRITTEN *just for you.*

God delights in you!

The LORD your God is with you...
He will take great delight in you.

ZEPHANIAH 3:17 NIV

For we are
his workmanship,
created in Christ Jesus
for good works.

EPHESIANS 2:10 ESV

THE CREATOR MADE YOU FOR HIS

Awesome Purpose

THE FUTURE IS AS

Bright

AS THE

PROMISES OF GOD.

—WILLIAM CAREY

GOD'S PROMISES
HAVE BEEN FULFILLED IN CHRIST
WITH A RESOUNDING
Yes!

II CORINTHIANS 1:20 NLT

God won't allow anything
to come to you
that hasn't first been screened
through His love.
Even challenges are
a time for seeking
His loving heart for you.

THERE IS A TIME FOR EVERYTHING,

AND A

Season

FOR EVERY ACTIVITY UNDER THE HEAVENS

...A TIME FOR LOVE.

ECCLESIASTES 3:1, 8 NIV

God's pursuit
of your heart
never stops.

God remains
the strength of my heart;
He is mine forever.

PSALM 73:26 NLT

Do you realize
how much you mean
to God?

This is how God showed
His love among us:
He sent His one and only Son
into the world that we might
live through Him.

1 JOHN 4:9 NIV

YOU ARE WILDLY LOVED.

We know how much God loves us,

and we have put our trust in His love.

God is love, and all who live in love

live in God, and God lives in them.

I JOHN 4:16 NLT

*My soul
finds rest
in God.*

PSALM 62:1 NIV

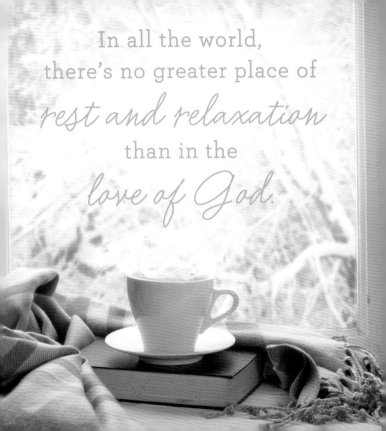

In all the world,
there's no greater place of
rest and relaxation
than in the
love of God.

Be still,
AND KNOW
THAT I AM
God

PSALM 46:10 NIV

BE STILL, AND KNOW

THAT HIS LOVE FOR YOU

IS COMPLETE.

His love is

unconditional.

GOD SHOWS HIS LOVE FOR US

ROMANS 5:8 ESV

When we live in God's love for us, we naturally *shine* with His beauty.

Those who look to Him are
radiant.

PSALM 34:5 NIV

AND WE KNOW THAT
GOD CAUSES EVERYTHING
TO WORK TOGETHER
FOR THE GOOD OF THOSE
WHO LOVE GOD AND ARE CALLED
ACCORDING TO HIS PURPOSE
FOR THEM.

ROMANS 8:28 NLT

YOUR LIFE'S

-AN-

Expression

OF *God's* GOOD-
NESS

No matter how deep
the valley,
God's love is deeper.

Who will
separate us
from the love
of Christ?

ROMANS 8:35 NASB

Your workmanship is

marvelous

how well I know it.

PSALM 139:14 NLT

God loves you
so much because
He knows you
so well.

you

WERE CALLED
TO

freedom

GALATIANS 5:13 ESV

Today

He wants to

fill your life

with joy and

free your heart

with love.

You could spend

your life

exploring God's love

and never reach

the end of it.

For the **LORD** the is good and His Love Endures forever...

PSALM 100:5 NIV

He Is
Faithful

1 John 1:9 NIV

The secret
to peace and rest
lies in God's
complete faithfulness.

FOR IT IS

GOD

WHO WORKS
IN YOU TO WILL
AND TO ACT
IN ORDER TO FULFILL
HIS GOOD PURPOSE.

PHILIPPIANS 2:13 NIV

GOD HAS
CALLED YOU
TO AN
INCREDIBLE
PURPOSE,
AND HE
BELIEVES
IN YOU.

Delight yourself in the Lord.

PSALM 37:4 ESV

Delighting in God
is His invitation
to know Him and His love.

For I am convinced that
neither death, nor life,
nor angels, nor principalities,
nor things present, nor things to come,
nor powers, nor height, nor depth,
nor any other created thing,
will be able to separate us
from the love of God,
which is in Christ Jesus our Lord.

ROMANS 8:38–39 NASB

NOTHING CAN SEPARATE YOU FROM

GOD'S OVERFLOWING

Love

Life is *Beautiful* because God is beautiful.

Oh, worship the LORD

in the beauty of holiness!

PSALM 96:9 NKJV

But not a single sparrow
can fall to the ground
without your Father knowing it.
And the very hairs on your head
are all numbered...
You are more valuable to God
than a whole flock of sparrows.

MATTHEW 10:29–31 NLT

God cares about
every detail
of your life.

Ask SEEK & Knock

{MATTHEW 7:7}

God meets you

where you are

&

takes you

where you need to go.

God is a changer.

He changes deserts...

...into places of rain.

He brings the oppressed...

...hope and life again.

He takes the old...

...and makes it new.

He turns your sorrows...

...into joys for you.

Therefore, if anyone is in Christ, he is a new creation. The old has passed away; ...the new has come.

2 CORINTHIANS 5:17 ESV

be strong
through the grace
God gives you

2 TIMOTHY 2:1 NLT

God's joy is your strength,

and His love is your shield.

You've got what it takes

to be amazing!

Everything beautiful

BEGINS WITH GOD.

He has MADE

EVERYTHING

beautiful

IN ITS TIME.

ECCLESIASTES 3:11 NIV

THE LORD LOOKS AT THE HEART

1 SAMUEL 16:7 NIV

What matters
is what's
on the inside.

True and lasting beauty is this—
the reflection of God's heart in
and through you.

THE DEFINITION
—of—
Lovely

IS BEING IN LOVE
with God.

I love You,

O LORD.

PSALM 18:1 NASB

You are a special
person created by an
awesome God.

God saw all that He had made, and it was very good.

GENESIS 1:31 NIV

God's beauty is found in
His heart...
My beauty is found in
HIM.

The unfading beauty of
a gentle and quiet spirit...
is of great worth in God's sight.

I PETER 3:4 NIV

You are valued & loved
just because
God made you!

God chose

You.

II THESSALONIANS 2:13 NLT

You are precious
and honored in
My sight, and...I love you.

ISAIAH 43:4 NIV

You knit me
together
in my mother's womb.

PSALM 139:13 NIV

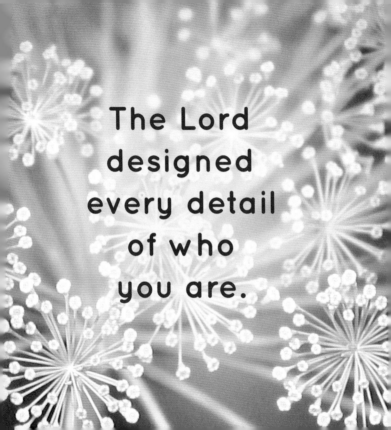

The Lord
designed
every detail
of who
you are.

THE HEAVENS DECLARE
the *Glory* of GOD
THE SKIES PROCLAIM THE
work of *His* hands.

PSALM 19:1 NIV

The beauty around you

is nothing compared to

God's beauty within you.

WONDERFULLY
made
AND
COMPLETELY
loved.

WE ARE GOD'S
masterpiece.

EPHESIANS 2:10 NLT

YOU ARE GOD'S

beautiful

treasure

God has chosen

you

to be His own special treasure.

DEUTERONOMY 7:6 NLT

GOD LOVES YOU
AND HAS CHOSEN YOU
TO BE HIS OWN.

1 THESSALONIANS 1:4 NLT

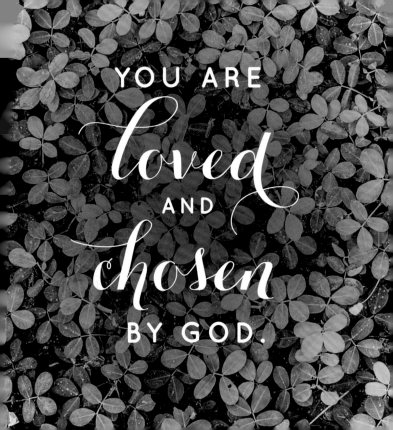

You are
ENJOYED, VALUED, & LOVED
just because you're YOU

He will take delight
in you with gladness.
With His love,
He will calm all your fears.
He will rejoice over you
with joyful songs.

ZEPHANIAH 3:17 NLT

God created
human beings
in His own image.

GENESIS 1:27 NLT

YOU WERE CREATED
IN THE
glorious
image
OF GOD.

Pursue inner beauty.

Charm is deceptive,
and beauty does not last;
but a woman who fears the LORD
will be greatly praised.

PROVERBS 31:30 NLT

I have loved you
with an everlasting love.

JEREMIAH 31:3 NIV

You
ARE
God's sweet
beautiful CREATION
& He loves you
with ALL His heart.

A happy heart
makes the face cheerful.

PROVERBS 15:13 NIV

The Lord
make His face shine
upon you and
be gracious to you.

NUMBERS 6:25 NIV

His grace shines
ON MY FACE AND THAT
makes me beautiful.

DaySpring

LIVE YOUR FAITH

Dear Friend,

This book was prayerfully crafted with you, the reader, in mind—every word, every sentence, every page—was thoughtfully written, designed, and packaged to encourage you...right where you are this very moment. At DaySpring, our vision is to see every person experience the life-changing message of God's love. So, as we worked through rough drafts, design changes, edits and details, we prayed for you to deeply experience His unfailing love, indescribable peace, and pure joy. It is our sincere hope that through these Truth-filled pages your heart will be blessed, knowing that God cares about you—your desires and disappointments, your challenges and dreams.

He knows. He cares. He loves you unconditionally.

BLESSINGS!
THE DAYSPRING BOOK TEAM